Contents

Contents 1

Introduction 4

Easy Toasts 5

Easy Banana Sandwich 5

Easy Marshmallow 6

Easy Peanut Butter Treat 6

Easy Turkey Stripes 7

Easy Crunch Mix 7

Easy Raspberry Ice Cream 8

Easy Fruit Sandwich 8

Easy Tortillas with Peanut Butter 9

Easy Parfait 9

Easy Snack 10

Easy Crackers Salad 10

Easy Homemade Sandwich 11

Easy Breakfast Mix 11

Easy Cheese Tortillas 12

Easy Granola Mix 12

Easy Potato Sticks 13

Easy Chicken Rolls 13

Easy Glazed Doughnut Holes 14

Peanut Butter & Honey Sandwich 14

Easy Cheesy Tortillas 15

Easy Batter 15

Easy Lemon Balls 16

Easy Salami Sandwich 16

Easy Frozen Banana 17

Easy Yogurt Parfaits 17

Easy Chicken Pitas 18

Frozen Bananas with Chocolate 18

Easy Cake Mix 19

Easy Bacon Salad 19

Easy Frozen Apples Chips 20

Easy Cheese Muffins 20

Easy Chicken Salad 21

Easy Garlic Toast 21

Easy Frozen Yogurt 22

Easy Fries 22

Easy Turkey Sandwich 23

Easy Ham Sandwich 23

Easy Yogurt with Pears 24

Easy Salami Sandwich 24

Easy Vegetable Sandwich 25

Easy Strawberry Breakfast 25

Easy Bacon Cream Cheese Breakfast 26

Easy Turkey Cream Cheese Breakfast 26

Easy Turkey Sandwich 27

Easy Avocado Tortillas 27

Tortillas with Turkey & Cherry 28

Easy Morning Sandwich 28

Easy Egg Sandwich 29

Easy Pizza 29

Easy Oatmeal 30

Easy Spiced Potato Fries 30

Easy Cheese Sandwich 31

Easy Toasts 31

Easy Roast Beef with Cheese 32

Easy Breakfast Pizza 32

Easy Chicken Sandwich 33

Easy Quick Sandwich 33

Easy Sausage Pizza 34

Easy Apple Sandwich 34

Easy Peach Sandwich 35

Easy Tuna Sandwich 35

Berry & Peach Salad 36

Tomato & Avocado Sandwich 36

Introduction

This book help your kids learn how to prepare their own food. During the day, children can cook whatever they want and perhaps even discover a new interest, and it is a great fun play. These easy 64 recipes your children can make all on their own.

Easy Toasts

Ingredients

- 6 slices white bread, toasted
- 6 tablespoons seedless raspberries jam
- 1 cup buttercream frosting
- 6 teaspoons edible glitter

Instructions

1. Over the toast, spread jam. Buttercream and edible glitter should be topped on the cake. Cut the toast into shapes or leave it whole.

Easy Banana Sandwich

Ingredients

- 4 slices whole wheat bread
- 1 banana, thinly sliced
- ¼ cup creamy peanut butter
- 2 tablespoons honey
- ¼ teaspoon ground cinnamon

Instructions

1. Mix peanut butter, honey and cinnamon. Spread over bread.
2. Slice the banana and layer it between two slices of bread.
3. Top with remaining bread.

Easy Marshmallow

Ingredients

- 1 package cream cheese, softened
- ¾ cup cherry yogurt
- 1 carton frozen whipped topping, thawed
- 1 jar marshmallow creme

Instructions

1. Cream cheese and yogurt should be beaten together in a large bowl.
2. Combine whipped topping and marshmallow creme in a mixing bowl.
3. Serve with fruit, to taste.

Easy Peanut Butter Treat

Ingredients

- ½ cup chunky peanut butter
- 3 tablespoons honey
- ½ teaspoon vanilla extract
- ¼ teaspoon ground cinnamon
- ½ cup nonfat dry milk powder
- ½ cup quick-cooking oats

Instructions

1. In a bowl, combine the peanut butter, honey, ground cinnamon and vanilla.
2. Combine the milk powder, oats, and crumbs of graham crackers. Shape into small balls.
3. Cover and refrigerate until serving.

Easy Turkey Stripes

Ingredients

- 1 cup sour cream
- 1 cup shredded cheddar cheese
- 4 cooked turkey strips, chopped
- 2 teaspoons sauce, to taste
- Hot cooked waffle-cut fries, to taste

Instructions

1. The first 4 ingredients mix in a bowl, until blended.
2. Serve with the waffle fries.

Easy Crunch Mix

Ingredients

- 2 cups plain crackers
- 1 cup mini pretzels
- 1 cup peanuts
- 1 cup chocolate-covered raisins
- 1 cup dried apricots

Instructions

1. In a bowl, combine all ingredients.
2. Be sure to store the container airtight.

Easy Raspberry Ice Cream

Ingredients

- 1 cup half-and-half cream
- ½ cup raspberries, fresh
- ¼ cup sugar
- 2 tablespoons honey
- 1 teaspoon vanilla extract

Instructions

1. Place the ingredients into a medium bowl.
2. Mix well all ingredients and pour into plastic cups and freeze in the freezer.

Easy Fruit Sandwich

Ingredients

- ½ cup peanut butter
- 6 slices white bread, toasted
- ¼ medium apple, thinly sliced
- ¼ medium banana, sliced
- ¼ medium avocado, sliced

Instructions

1. Spread peanut butter on bread and top with apple, banana and avocado slices.

Easy Tortillas with Peanut Butter

Ingredients

- 4 tablespoons peanut butter
- 2 flour tortillas
- 2 teaspoons honey
- ½ cup dried apricots

Instructions

1. Spread peanut butter over each tortilla.
2. Drizzle with honey and sprinkle with dried apricots, roll them up and cut into slices.

Easy Parfait

Ingredients

- 2 cups fat-free vanilla yogurt
- 1 medium peach, chopped
- 1 cup fresh blackberries
- ½ cup granola with raisins
- 1 cup fresh raspberries
- ¼ cup sugar

Instructions

1. Mix yogurt and sugar together.
2. Layer the yogurt, peach, blackberries, raspberries, and granola into some glasses. Repeat layers.

Easy Snack

Ingredients

- 1 package pretzels, to taste
- 1 can cashews
- 1 package cheddar crackers
- Spices, to taste
- ¼ cup sunflower oil
- 3 tablespoons scallions, chopped

Instructions

1. In a bowl, combine the pretzels, cashews, crackers, and spices, toss gently to combine.
2. Drizzle with oil, add scallions and toss until well mix.

Easy Crackers Salad

Ingredients

- 1 tablespoon canola oil
- 1 prepackaged salad mix
- 2 packages oyster crackers

Instructions

1. In a small bowl, mix the oil and the salad dressing mix.
2. In a large bowl, mix the crackers and the salad mixture over the crackers.
3. Allow to stand at least 15 min before serving.

Easy Homemade Sandwich

Ingredients

- ½ cup mayonnaise
- 8 lettuce leaves
- 8 thin slices fully cooked ham
- 8 thin slices tomato
- 8 slices white bread, toasted

Instructions

1. Spread the mayonnaise on each slice of bread.
2. Place lettuce leaves, tomato and ham on each slice of bread.

Easy Breakfast Mix

Ingredients

- 1 package apple-nut granola
- 1 package raisins
- 1 package milk chocolate M&M's
- 1 can sweet roasted peanuts
- 1 package dried apricots

Instructions

1. All ingredients should be placed in a large bowl and tossed together.
2. Keep airtight.

Easy Cheese Tortillas

Ingredients

- 4 flour tortillas, room temperature
- 1 large tomato, thinly sliced
- 1 medium red pepper, cut into thin strips
- 1 cup shredded lettuce
- 1 cup smoked cheese, to taste
- ½ cup ranch salad dressing

Instructions

1. Place some ingredients on each tortilla. Layer with tomato, red pepper, lettuce and cheese.
2. Drizzle with salad dressing. Roll up tightly.

Easy Granola Mix

Ingredients

- 1 package chocolate chips
- 1 cup raisins
- 1 cup banana-nut granola

Instructions

1. All ingredients should be placed in a large bowl and tossed together.
2. Keep airtight.

Easy Potato Sticks

Ingredients

- ¼ cup honey
- 1 cup creamy peanut butter
- 1 can potato sticks

Instructions

1. In a bowl, melt honey and peanut butter. Stir until smooth.
2. Stir in potato sticks gently.
3. Drop mixture onto the baking sheet. Refrigerate 20-25 minutes or until set.

Easy Chicken Rolls

Ingredients

- 1 can white chicken, drained
- 1 carton cream cheese, to taste
- ½ cup ketchup
- 6 flour tortillas, to taste
- 6 lettuce leaves
- 6 red bell pepper rings

Instructions

1. Mix chicken, cream cheese and ketchup, then spread over tortillas.
2. Add lettuce leaves and bell pepper rings. Next, roll up tightly.

Easy Glazed Doughnut Holes

Ingredients

- 2 cups confectioners' sugar
- 1 tablespoon thawed raspberries juice concentrate
- 1 tablespoon thawed cherry juice concentrate
- 2 tablespoons lemon juice
- 14 doughnut holes

Instructions

1. Whisk together sugar, lemon juice and juice concentrate to achieve until smooth.
2. Dip doughnut holes in the glaze and transfer to waxed paper. Let stand until set.

Peanut Butter & Honey Sandwich

Ingredients

- 2 peanut butter sandwiches
- 2 honey & butter sandwiches
- 1 apple, sliced

Instructions

1. Cut sandwiches into small squares.
2. Alternately thread grapes, sandwich squares and banana slices onto each skewer. Serve immediately.

Easy Cheesy Tortillas

Ingredients

- 4 flour tortillas, warmed
- 1cup shredded cheddar cheese
- ½ cup sour cream
- 1 tablespoon mayonnaise

Instructions

1. Place the tortillas on waxed paper. Combine the cheese, sour cream and mayonnaise, then spread over half of each tortilla. Roll up tortillas.
2. Fry in a skillet over medium heat for 2 minutes on each side, or until golden brown.

Easy Batter

Ingredients

- 1 package cream cheese, softened
- ¼ cup butter, softened
- ¼ cup baking cocoa
- ¼ cup milk
- 2 tablespoons sugar
- mini chocolate chips to top

Instructions

1. In a bowl, beat cream cheese and butter until smooth.
2. Beat in cocoa, milk, and sugar until smooth. Sprinkle with chocolate chips.

Easy Lemon Balls

Ingredients

- 1 package cream cheese, softened
- 1 cup crushed cookies, to taste
- 1 cup graham cracker crumbs
- 1 cup powdered sugar, divided
- 2 tablespoons lemon juice
- ¼ cup coconut flakes

Instructions

1. In a bowl, beat cream cheese, cookies, cracker crumbs, powdered sugar, and lemon juice until blended.
2. Shape into a small ball and place on a plate. Sprinkle with coconut.

Easy Salami Sandwich

Ingredients

- 6 slices toast
- 2 tablespoons pasta sauce
- 2 tablespoons mayonnaise
- 6 slices cheese, to taste
- 12 slices thin salami

Instructions

1. Preheat the oven to 300°F. Add the toast; cook until lightly browned, about 4 minutes per side.
2. Mix the pasta sauce and mayonnaise. Spread all 6 toasts with the sauce and mayonnaise mixture.
3. Top with cheese and salami.

Easy Frozen Banana

Ingredients

- ½ cup banana yogurt
- ½ cup apple yogurt
- 2 cups fruity cereal, to taste
- 4 medium bananas, peeled and cut in half crosswise
- 8 wooden pop sticks

Instructions

1. Place yogurt and cereal in the medium bowl. Insert wooden sticks through bananas.
2. Roll bananas in cereal after dipping them in yogurt.
3. On a waxed paper-lined baking sheet, transfer the bananas.
4. Freeze until firm, about 1 hour.

Easy Yogurt Parfaits

Ingredients

- 1 cup sweetened pear sauce
- vanilla sugar, to taste
- ½ cup granola with raisins
- 1 ½ cups vanilla yogurt

Instructions

1. In a bowl, combine pear sauce and vanilla sugar.
2. 4 parfait glasses need to be filled with 1 tablespoon of granola each. Layer each with ½ cup yogurt and ¼ cup pear sauce.

Easy Chicken Pitas

Ingredients

- 1 cup cubed boiled chicken
- ½ cup chopped celery
- ½ cup unsweetened crushed pineapple, well drained
- ¼ cup mayonnaise
- 1 small onion, chopped
- Salt, to taste
- 5 pita pocket halves

Instructions

1. Combine chicken, celery, pineapple, mayonnaise, onion, and salt.
2. Chicken mixture should be filled into pita halves.

Frozen Bananas with Chocolate

Ingredients

- 3 bananas
- 1 cup milk chocolate chips
- 1 tablespoon shortening
- ½ cup peanuts, chopped
- ½ cup sweetened coconut flakes

Instructions

1. Cut bananas into slices. Transfer to a plate and freeze until completely firm, about 2 hours.
2. Melt chocolate chips and shortening and stir until smooth.
3. Drizzle bananas with chocolate mixture. Top with peanuts and coconut flakes. Freeze at least 25 minutes.

Easy Cake Mix

Ingredients

- 1 cake mix, to taste
- 1 small egg
- ½ cup milk
- ½ cup sunflower oil
- ½ cup raisins
- 1 cup baking chips, to taste
- ¼ cup coconut flakes

Instructions

1. Preheat oven to 350°. In a bowl, combine cake mix, egg, milk, raisins and oil. Stir in baking chips and coconut flakes. Grease a baking pan with oil.
2. Bake 20-22 minutes, or until a toothpick is clean. Set aside and cool completely in pan.

Easy Bacon Salad

Ingredients

- 15 fully cooked bacon strips
- 1 cup lettuce, chopped
- ½ cup tomatoes, chopped
- ½ cup cheese, to taste, shredded
- ½ cup salad dressing, to taste
- Salt, to taste

Instructions

1. Place bacon strips, lettuce, tomatoes, cheese, and salt into a bowl. Mix it all together.
2. Drizzle with salad dressing. Serve.

Easy Frozen Apples Chips

Ingredients

- 2 cups apple chips
- ½ cup milk chocolate chips
- 1 teaspoon shortening

Instructions

1. Arrange apple chips in a single layer on a plate.
2. Melt chocolate chips and shortening, and stir until smooth. Next, drizzle chocolate mixture over chips. Freeze about 15 minutes, or until set.

Easy Cheese Muffins

Ingredients

- 1 package muffin mix, to taste
- ½ cup milk
- 1 egg
- ½ cup cheese, to taste, shredded
- Salt, to taste
- Ground black pepper, to taste

Instructions

1. Preheat oven to 350°. Grease oil 9 nonstick muffin cups.
2. In a bowl, combine muffin mix, milk, egg, cheese, salt, and pepper. Fill prepared muffin cups.
3. Bake 15-20 minutes, or until a toothpick is clean. Set aside and cool completely in pan.

Easy Chicken Salad

Ingredients

- ½ cup mayonnaise
- ½ cup finely chopped celery
- Salt, to taste
- 2 hard-boiled large eggs, minced
- 2 cups chopped cooked chicken breast
- 3 lettuce leaves

Instructions

1. Mix all ingredients, salted. Salad is ready.

Easy Garlic Toast

Ingredients

- 1 package garlic Texas toast
- ½ cup ketchup
- 1 package sliced salami
- 1 cup mozzarella cheese, shredded

Instructions

1. Preheat oven to 400°. Place toast in a baking pan. Bake 4-5 minutes.
2. Spread the toasts with ketchup.
3. Top with salami and mozzarella. Bake until mozzarella is melted, about 5 minutes.

Easy Frozen Yogurt

Ingredients

- 2 cups fat-free Greek yogurt
- 1 cup fresh strawberries, chopped
- 1 tablespoon sugar
- Vanilla extract, to taste

Instructions

1. Fill the cup with about ½ cup yogurt.
2. Mix strawberries, vanilla and sugar in a food processor.
3. Spoon strawberries mixture into each cup. Stir gently. Freeze until firm.

Easy Fries

Ingredients

- 1 package frozen steak fries
- ¼ cup milk
- ½ teaspoon garlic powder
- ¼ teaspoon onion powder
- Salt, to taste

Instructions

1. Bake the steak fries at 450° for 20 minutes, or until tender and golden brown.
2. In a bowl, combine the milk, salt, garlic powder and onion powder. Drizzle over fries.

Easy Turkey Sandwich

Ingredients

- 4 slices whole wheat bread
- 2 slices thinly sliced deli turkey
- 2 slices tomato
- 2 slices cheese
- 2 teaspoons salted butter, softened
- 2 slices bell pepper

Instructions

1. In a skillet, toast bread over medium heat until golden brown, 3-4 minutes per side. Cool.
2. Spread butter on 2 bread slices. Top with turkey, tomato, cheese and bell pepper. Top with the remaining 2 slices of bread.

Easy Ham Sandwich

Ingredients

- 4 slices whole wheat bread
- 2 slices ham, to taste
- 2 slices cucumber
- 2 slices cheese
- 2 teaspoons salted butter, softened
- 2 slices bell pepper

Instructions

1. In a skillet, toast bread over medium heat until golden brown, 3-4 minutes per side. Cool.
2. Spread butter on 2 bread slices. Top with ham, cucumber, cheese and bell pepper. Top with the remaining 2 slices of bread.

Easy Yogurt with Pears

Ingredients

- 4 cups cut-up fresh pears
- 1 cup vanilla yogurt
- 1 tablespoon honey
- Almond extract, to taste
- Vanilla extract, to taste

Instructions

1. Divide pears among some individual serving bowls.
2. Combine the yogurt, honey and extracts, then spoon over the pears.

Easy Salami Sandwich

Ingredients

- 4 slices whole wheat bread
- 2 slices salami
- 2 lettuce leaves
- 2 slices cheese
- 2 teaspoons salted butter, softened
- 2 slices bell pepper

Instructions

1. In a skillet, toast bread over medium heat until golden brown, 3-4 minutes per side. Cool.

2. Spread butter on 2 bread slices. Top with salami, lettuce, cheese and bell pepper. Top with the remaining 2 slices of bread.

Easy Vegetable Sandwich

Ingredients

- 4 slices whole wheat bread
- 2 slices tomato
- 2 slices cucumber
- 2 slices cheese
- 2 teaspoons salted butter, softened
- 2 slices bell pepper

Instructions

1. In a skillet, toast bread over medium heat until golden brown, 3-4 minutes per side. Cool.
2. Spread butter on 2 bread slices. Top with tomato, cucumber, cheese and bell pepper. Top with the remaining 2 slices of bread.

Easy Strawberry Breakfast

Ingredients

- 1 cup fresh strawberries, quartered
- 4 flour tortillas
- ½ cup cream cheese, softened
- 1 tablespoon honey
- ½ cup yogurt, to taste

Instructions

1. In a skillet, toast tortillas over medium heat until golden brown, 1-2 minutes per side. Transfer to the plate.
2. Beat together cream cheese, honey and yogurt until blended. Spread tortillas with cream cheese mixture and top with strawberries.

Easy Bacon Cream Cheese Breakfast

Ingredients

- 1 cup cream cheese, softened
- 2 tablespoons finely onion, chopped
- 1 teaspoon milk
- 8 bacon strips, chopped
- Salt, to taste

Instructions

1. Preheat oven to 375°.
2. In a small bowl, mix cream cheese, onion, salt, milk and bacon until blended.
3. Pour the mixture into a baking dish.
4. Bake 12-15 minutes or until golden brown. Cool.

Easy Turkey Cream Cheese Breakfast

Ingredients

- 1 cup cream cheese, softened
- ¼ teaspoon pepper
- 8 slices white bread
- ¾ pound sliced deli turkey
- 2 tablespoons butter, softened

Instructions

1. In a bowl, beat the cream cheese and pepper until combined.
2. Spread over 4 slices of bread. Top with turkey and remaining bread. Spread butter over both sides of sandwiches.
3. Bake in a grill until golden brown, 2-4 minutes.

Easy Turkey Sandwich

Ingredients

- 8 slices white bread
- 4 slices tomato
- 4 slices cheese, to taste, quartered
- 4 cooked bacon strips
- 4 slices deli turkey
- 4 lettuce leaves
- 4 slices medium ripe avocado

Instructions

1. Fill each slice of bread with tomato, cheese, bacon, turkey, lettuce and avocado in any order. Covered on top with the remaining piece of bread.

Easy Avocado Tortillas

Ingredients

- 1 tablespoon oil, to taste
- 12 corn tortillas
- 2 cups cheese, to taste, shredded
- 2 boiled eggs, shredded
- 1 ripe avocado, sliced

Instructions

1. Grease a griddle with oil and heat over medium heat.
2. Place 6 tortillas on griddle, then top with cheese, eggs and avocado. Top with remaining tortillas.
3. Cook until tortillas are lightly browned and cheese is melted, 4-5 minutes on each side.

Tortillas with Turkey & Cherry

Ingredients

- 3 tablespoons cherry jam
- ½ cup reduced-fat cream cheese
- 4 whole wheat tortillas
- 4 slices reduced-sodium deli turkey

Instructions

1. In a bowl, mix cream cheese and jam. Spread mixture over each tortilla. Layer with turkey. Roll up tightly.

Easy Morning Sandwich

Ingredients

- 4 slices whole wheat bread
- 2 slices cheese
- 2 teaspoons salted butter, softened
- 2 slices bell pepper
- 1 fried egg

Instructions

1. In a skillet, toast bread over medium heat until golden brown, 3-4 minutes per side. Cool.
2. Spread butter on 2 bread slices. Top with egg, cheese and bell pepper. Top with the remaining 2 slices of bread.

Easy Egg Sandwich

Ingredients

- 4 piece fried bacon
- 1 fried egg
- 1 tablespoon ketchup
- 1 tablespoon cheddar cheese, shredded
- 4 slices whole wheat bread

Instructions

1. In a skillet, toast bread over medium heat until golden brown, 3-4 minutes per side. Cool.
2. Spread ketchup on 2 bread slices. Top with bacon, egg, and cheese. Top with remaining 2 slices of bread.

Easy Pizza

Ingredients

- 1 prebaked 12-inch pizza crust
- 1 tablespoon olive oil
- 1 tablespoon ketchup
- 1 cup cooked shredded turkey
- ½ cup bell pepper, chopped
- ½ cup olives, chopped
- 1 cup shredded cheese, to taste

Instructions

1. Preheat oven to 450°. Place crust on an ungreased pizza pan. Brush with oil.
2. Spread ketchup over crust. Top with turkey, bell pepper, olives and cheese.
3. Bake until cheese is melted, 10-15 minutes.

Easy Oatmeal

Ingredients

- 1 ½ cups water
- 1 cup old-fashioned oats
- 2 tablespoons honey
- ¼ teaspoon ground cinnamon
- 1 chopped apple

Instructions

1. In a saucepan, bring water to boil. Stir in the oats and cook 7 minutes over medium heat.
2. Transfer oatmeal to bowls and add honey, cinnamon and apple. Serve.

Easy Spiced Potato Fries

Ingredients

- 1 package frozen french-fried potatoes
- ½ teaspoon garlic powder
- ½ teaspoon pepper
- Salt, to taste

Instructions

1. Preheat oven. Bake fries according to package directions.
2. In a bowl, combine the remaining ingredients. Sprinkle over fries. Cook.

Easy Cheese Sandwich

Ingredients

- 4 slices whole wheat bread
- 2 slices cheese
- 2 teaspoons butter, softened
- 2 slices bell pepper

Instructions

1. In a skillet, toast bread over medium heat until golden brown, 3-4 minutes per side. Cool.
2. Spread butter on 2 bread slices. Top with cheese and bell pepper. Top with the remaining two slices of bread.

Easy Toasts

Ingredients

- 4 slices toast
- 2 large eggs
- ½ cup milk
- 1 tablespoon maple syrup
- ¼ teaspoon ground cinnamon

Instructions

1. Cut each piece of bread into small pieces; place in a dish.
2. In a bowl, whisk eggs, milk, syrup and cinnamon. Pour over bread. Place in a greased baking pan.
3. Preheat oven to 350°. Place the toasts in the oven. Cook for 5 minutes, then turn and cook until golden brown.

Easy Roast Beef with Cheese

Ingredients

- 6 slices provolone cheese
- 6 slices deli roast beef
- ½ cup finely chopped sweet red pepper

Instructions

1. Preheat oven to 375°. Grease a baking dish with butter. Top with roast beef, cheese and red pepper.
2. Bake until cheese is golden brown and melted, about 15 minutes. Serve.

Easy Breakfast Pizza

Ingredients

- 1 tube refrigerated pizza crust
- 1 tablespoon olive oil, divided
- 1 package bacon bits
- 1 cup shredded cheese, to taste

Instructions

1. Preheat oven to 400°. Unroll and press dough of a greased pan. Brush with oil. Bake until lightly browned, about 6 minutes.
2. Sprinkle the pizza crust with bacon bits and cheeses.
3. Bake until cheese is melted, about 7 minutes.

Easy Chicken Sandwich

Ingredients

- 4 slices sourdough bread
- 2 tablespoons mayonnaise
- ½ cup cheese, to taste
- ½ teaspoon ketchup
- 2 slices boiled chicken
- 2 slices mozzarella cheese

Instructions

1. In a skillet, toast bread over medium heat until golden brown, 3-4 minutes per side. Cool.
2. In a bowl, combine mayonnaise, cheese and ketchup, then spread over 2 bread slices. Top with chicken and mozzarella cheese. Top with the remaining 2 slices of bread.

Easy Quick Sandwich

Ingredients

- 4 slices bread, to taste
- 2 tablespoons mayonnaise
- ½ cup cheese, to taste
- 2 slices boiled chicken
- 2 slices salami

Instructions

1. In a skillet, toast bread over medium heat until golden brown, 3-4 minutes per side. Cool.
2. In a bowl, combine mayonnaise and cheese, then spread over 2 bread slices. Top with chicken and salami. Top with the remaining 2 slices of bread.

Easy Sausage Pizza

Ingredients

- 1 pizza crust
- 1 cup shredded cheese, to taste
- 10 slices sausage, to taste
- ½ cup finely chopped sweet red pepper
- ½ teaspoon ketchup

Instructions

1. Place the pizza crust on a baking tray, spread ketchup on it. Top with cheese, sausage and pepper.
2. Bake in a preheated oven until golden brown, and cheese melted, about 10-15 minutes.

Easy Apple Sandwich

Ingredients

- 4 slices whole wheat bread
- 1 apple, thinly sliced
- ¼ cup creamy peanut butter
- 2 tablespoons honey
- ¼ teaspoon ground cinnamon

Instructions

1. Mix peanut butter, honey and cinnamon. Spread over bread.
2. Slice apple and layer it between two slices of bread.
3. Top with remaining bread.

Easy Peach Sandwich

Ingredients

- 4 slices whole wheat bread
- 1 peach, thinly sliced
- ¼ cup creamy peanut butter
- 2 tablespoons honey
- ¼ teaspoon ground cinnamon

Instructions

1. Mix peanut butter, honey and cinnamon. Spread over bread.
2. Slice peach and layer it between two slices of bread.
3. Top with remaining bread.

Easy Tuna Sandwich

Ingredients

- ½ cup light tuna in water
- 1 fried egg
- 4 slices whole wheat bread

Instructions

1. In a skillet, toast bread over medium heat until golden brown, 3-4 minutes per side. Cool.
2. Spread tuna on two bread slices. Top with egg. Top with remaining 2 slices of bread.

Berry & Peach Salad

Ingredients

- 2 medium peaches, sliced
- Sugar, to taste
- ½ teaspoon lemon juice
- ½ cup cream cheese
- 1 cup fresh blueberries

Instructions

1. In a bowl, mix peaches with sugar and lemon juice.
2. Gradually beat peaches and cream cheese. Gently combine peaches and blueberries.

Tomato & Avocado Sandwich

Ingredients

- ½ avocado, peeled and mashed
- 4 slices whole wheat bread, toasted
- ½ medium tomato, sliced
- ¼ cup butter

Instructions

1. Spread avocado and tomato over 2 slices of toast. Spread butter over remaining 2 toast slices and place on top of avocado toast.

Made in the USA
Thornton, CO
08/18/23 04:19:42

4505ae5f-2939-447e-8440-99850705f984R02